When Love Hurts and

Everything Turns to SH#T

How To Rebuild a Broken Heart When You Can't Even

Find the Pieces

By Simeon Lindstrom

Table Of Contents

Introduction

If you've found yourself thinking "could this really be happening to me?" a lot recently, then this book was written for you!

Infidelity is a strange thing: it seems like it's all around us all the time, but when it happens *to us*, we're horrified and can't believe it. Could this really be happening?

When you watch a movie and see the stereotypical angry husband burst in through the door and catch his cheating wife in the act, you feel bad for him. But unless you've actually had this experience yourself, you might not understand just how truly upsetting it can be. If you're reading this book, there's a strong chance that the reality of being cheated on is hitting you ...and it's harder than it looks! After all, the one person who you might have chosen to confide in after such a painful experience is the very person who caused the pain.

The angry guy in the movie doesn't quite show the whole picture. When your partner is unfaithful, you may feel angry, humiliated, sad, numb, brimming with murderous rage, confusion or any awful blend of all of those. And all in the few minutes it takes for the realization to dawn on you. And then you have to keep going to work, doing your chores and getting on with life ...or what you *thought* was your life!

When I think of this kind of thing, I imagine a happy, contented person at a big table, building an enormous jigsaw puzzle. Not just any jigsaw, but a really massive, complex one, the kind that takes weeks to build. You've got the end result in your mind's eye, you've built the corners and edges, and best of all, you have your closest friend and fellow puzzle builder with you: your partner. You're both plugging away at building this beautiful puzzle, together. Then one day, they get up, turn the table over and send every last piece spilling across the floor. Days and days of work, gone. Those four precious corners, lost in the mess. The picture that you were building, together, now lay broken on the floor.

Why would anybody do such a thing? Weren't they working on the puzzle *with* you? For a moment, you stand and look at the mess on the floor and ask yourself (you guessed it) "is this really happening right now?" And before you've made sense of the whole incident, your partner is standing in front of you, crying and pleading for forgiveness. "Please try to understand!" they say, "please don't be angry. Think about how hard it's been for me, let me explain..."

When someone cheats in a relationship, your whole world can turn upside down overnight. The "picture" you were building together, as a team, is thrown out the window. Now what?

I should mention now that this book is not about how to *leave* someone after they've been unfaithful to you. Some people have a zero tolerance policy for it, or they're not invested enough to take on the work required to trust again, or the cheating is really just the end of a relationship that has run its course anyway.

Nobody is entitled to forgiveness after a deception. For some relationships, the deception is so deep, so lasting and so pervasive that there really isn't much to do except separate as gracefully as possible.

But cheating doesn't *have to* be the end of the world. This book is for those people who want to know how to keep going anyway. If you've recently experienced the soul-crushing realization that your partner hasn't been faithful, it might seem strange to hear that in a way, cheating can be a *good* thing. Even though you might feel your heart and mind pulled in a million different directions right now, my hope is that by the end of this book, you have found a new clarity, a fresh calm, and a clear sense of how to move forward.

With compassion, self-awareness and concrete commitment, a relationship can survive any disaster. Even cheating. Of course, the hard part is finding out how to be compassionate, self-aware and committed!

So, your partner cheated. They lied to you, broke a promise and reached out to someone else for attention or sex or love. And you're devastated. But if the cat's out of the bag and your partner is in front of you, begging for forgiveness and another chance, then this book will show you what that actually means.

Your puzzle is broken now. But it IS possible to sit down again, together, and rebuild. It IS possible for your partner to change, for your relationship to change and more importantly, for things to get *better*.

Your new puzzle probably won't be of the same picture anymore, and you'll probably have to go more slowly and carefully when you build it. But it can be done. The new picture can be just as beautiful as the old one ...or even more so.

Chapter 1: Ground Zero: The Day your World Changes

I call the moment when you discover the infidelity "ground zero" because it can feel like your heart has just been blasted with a nuclear bomb. Whether you've had your suspicions or it came completely from nowhere, staring at hard evidence can be a real blow. Some people discover incriminating photos or texts, others hear a confession and others, like our movie man above, discover the act itself.

Cheating hurts so much for two key reasons, and it's these reasons that makes it different from other kinds of trauma you could experience.

It hurts because it comes from the person you love

We expect murderers to murder, and we know that politicians lie. We are of course affected when people we don't like do something to harm us ...but we expect it. What we don't expect is that our partners – the people we associate with love and security and intimacy and safety – can be a source of pain. The anguish of seeing someone who used to give you so much happiness flip and turn into someone who gives you pain can be disorienting to say the least. When someone hurts you, you've gained a problem. But when *someone you love* hurts you, that's two problems: the hurt they've given you, plus the fact that now you have one less loving, supportive person in your life.

It hurts because of the sexual element

One of the most fundamental parts of sexual intimacy is that it's (usually! Although I'm not judging!) just two people, alone, shutting out the rest of the world and enjoying one another in private. We mark the beginning of a more serious relationship by expecting and committing to sexual exclusivity.

For many people, exclusivity is the defining feature of a relationship. So when that exclusivity is yanked away, it can feel like the whole relationship "is a lie". It's not rational, but the sexual element makes this kind of betrayal so much worse. You feel exposed, cheapened and deeply threatened. It goes a little deeper than jealousy though. It can be a massive shock to realize that you're not The One but One of Many.

It might sound strange, but realizing that you are not the only person that your partner finds attractive can unlock strong emotions that go right back to childhood. When we come into this world, we are perfectly fused with our mothers. In our still-developing minds, love = survival. Literally. Because we're completely helpless, her love and care literally translates to us being able to survive and thrive.

If you've seen how jealous a toddler can get when a second baby enters the family picture, you'll understand how painful it can be to learn that you're not The One, but One of Many. As we grow up, we learn to take turns, and to share. But there's still a little part of us that remembers how amazing it felt to be the center of the universe, to have someone's full love and attention, all for ourselves. For many people, romantic relationships are a place to recreate that warm feeling, if only temporarily. We close the door on the world. It's "just the two of us". "Love chemicals" like oxytocin are released when a mother bonds with her baby ...and when two lovers stare into each other's eyes and forget about everyone else. You love them and they love you and it feels warm and safe and wonderful.

And then they cheat.

If we've learnt in childhood that love = survival, then losing that
love can literally feel as though our survival is threatened. It can
feel like the end of the world. Rejection and deception of this kind
isn't like getting fired or failing at a project. It cuts to the very core
of who we are, of the fundamental hope that keeps all of us going:
that we are lovable and deserve to be cared for, and to live. Getting
cheated on can feel like getting kicked out of the nest and left to die
in the cold. I know I'm being dramatic, but feeling like this is not
melodrama – it's rooted in the realities of the way our brains work.

The hours and days after you discover an infidelity are going to be
chaotic.

Before we continue with the rest of this book, it's important to
understand exactly what things are happening inside you, and why.
How would you react if you were kissing your partner and they
suddenly turned into a ferocious tiger in your arms? Well, that's
essentially what *did* happen, according to your brain!

What to expect when your heart's been ripped out and stomped on

Forgive the dramatic title, but as you'll see, hyperbole is also part of a normal response! After an infidelity, all of the following are perfectly normal:

- You're totally numb and don't feel anything.
- You're having trouble thinking clearly or sticking to one train of thought.
- You're mad as hell and feel yourself losing your temper all the time.
- You want cold, hard revenge and you've fantasized about getting even.
- You're sadder than you've ever felt. You feel hopeless, and wonder what the point is.
- You feel paranoid – if people can lie about this, what else is a lie?
- You feel humiliated and like you've been made a fool of. You wonder if people are laughing at your expense.
- You're confused. You just can't reconcile how happy everything seemed with this ugly new piece of information. You really don't get it: *why*?
- You're disappointed, and feel a tired, old cynicism creeping in. How could you be so stupid to trust someone?

- You feel like you just want to run away and never deal with any of it.

- You feel kind of relieved.

All of these emotions (even the last one!) are perfectly normal reactions to being cheated on. You might feel completely awful and unable to function some days, and others you can almost forget about your feelings for a while and get on with life like nothing happened. It's also normal to swing wildly from one emotion to another.

What do you do with this hurricane going on in your head?

Well, nothing. That's right, you just let it be. The most important thing to keep reminding yourself of in the early days is that you don't *have to* feel like anything.

Give yourself permission to feel ...whatever it is you feel.

Your partner may be pressuring you to talk immediately, or to forgive, or to explain and tell them what you think, and what you'll do and why. As kindly as possible, ask them to give you time. If you're like most people, you won't be in a state of mind to deal with any of that. Your first task is to take care of yourself and make sure you're processing all your emotions responsibly.

So, what does that look like?

Take care of the physical stuff

Anchor yourself in the routine of your life. You still need to eat, to run errands and to work. You don't need to force yourself to do things you can't, but don't abandon important routines like good eating and getting adequate sleep.

In fact, you might find it very soothing to just "unplug" for a second and immerse in some quiet task, alone. Have a bath, go for a long walk, read a book you like or get your hair done. Communicate to your body and mind: "you are cared for!" Take your vitamins, keep up your exercise routine and try not to do any serious overeating or drinking, no matter how appealing it might seem!

Avoid making any big decisions

Let's go back to our movie guy. After he discovers his cheating wife, he might jump into his car, drive off in a huff and file for divorce the next day. While this is certainly an option, it's usually better to give yourself time to cool off before going nuclear. You may still make the same decision you would have in the heat of the moment, but you'll feel better about things and more in control if you slow down and give yourself time to process.

Chapter 2: Now What? A Decision You Never Asked to Make

It's kind of irritating, when you think of it. Here you are, minding your own business, and your partner drops this huge, awkward, ugly thing in your lap. It's like they're saying, "Here, you figure it out!".

They broke things, it seems, and now you get the privilege of fixing them!

The ball is, as they say, in your court. And you might not like that it is. The assumption is always that the cheater is remorseful, and that the person who was deceived is now in a possession to decide whether they'll forgive or not. Even if it's never laid out this way, the fact is that there will be lines drawn separating out "good guy" and "bad guy" in your situation, and as the good guy, you'll be expected to have an opinion, and to act on it first.

If you've followed the advice of the previous chapter, you've given yourself the gift of letting your emotions cool down a bit so that you can handle the situation with more clarity. Whether this takes you a day or a week or even longer, you're stuck with this question: now what?

I'm a firm believer in being positive and expecting the best when it comes to relationships. Really. But with cheating, you need to moderate that positivity with a healthy dose of reality. Cheating is a problem. A big one. In this book, I want to show you that it can transform from being a problem into being an *opportunity*, and a chance for growth and insight and yes, deeper love.

But that transformation doesn't happen by itself!

Infidelity can be the start of something new and genuine and real – but only under the right conditions.

Before you pour yourself into the project of healing after the betrayal and rebuilding that beautiful jigsaw again, you need to be realistic. Below, I'm outlining three key conditions that need to exist in order for a relationship to survive and thrive after an infidelity.

Condition one: the deception is not ongoing

The first condition for healing a relationship is, obviously, that the deceit that caused the trouble has to actually *end*. Healing can only happen once the pain totally and completely stops. Before you climb the mountain of building trust again, you need to actively start at zero again, where there might not be trust, but there are also no fresh infringements, no new lies.

There are many ways that infidelity can be discovered and wrangled with, all the while not *technically* being dealt with properly. For example, your partner could be "drip feeding" you the truth. Let me explain: you discover a damning text to a work colleague and ask them about it. They deny it for a week, then admit that yes, something was going on, but isn't anymore. You're hurt, so you ask if there's anything else. Was it ever physical? How often did it happen? They say, yes it was physical, but just once. And it happened weeks ago. You push for more details. How often were you in contact? They say only once in a while, but they don't mention emails, only face-to-face contact. They don't tell you about the emails because you didn't ask. But you ask them later, and they deny it at first, but finally admit it. You ask, how many emails, and they say, just one, but later you find out...

As you can see, this kind of thing can make you tear your hair out. To their credit, your partner might be so horrified about what will happen when you know the full extent of the betrayal that they believe they're protecting themselves and you by "softening" the truth. So they feed you the information, bit by bit. Actually, from your side, this looks even worse: are they going to lie about every little thing? Do you have to *drag* it out of them?

Everyone's situation is different, but in order to move forward and heal, you'll have to be deadly honest and real with each other. And the first step to this is knowing what actually happened. You don't need to know every sickening detail, but what is important is this: is your partner forthcoming with information?

Really think about it. The person who comes running to you after a single mistake and tells you everything without prompting is different from the person who was "caught" and forced to confess.

The way that your partner talks to you about the infidelity is very telling, so listen:

Is their attitude one of "coming clean", of telling without prompting and of wanting to level with you as soon as possible? This person has deceived you, but the deception is not ongoing. On the other hand, are they "drip feeding" the truth to you, lying by omission, minimizing their actions or giving information only when pushed for it? This person has deceived you, and they are actively in a mindset that is *not* truthful and open, right now. Pay attention.

Condition two: your partner is remorseful

Almost always, the cheater is going to be "sorry". But again, listen carefully to the nature of this apology and what it really means. Where this sorry comes from could spell the difference between moving on in love and pursuing a relationship that is not worth your time and trust.

Remorse means that the person deeply, truly understands that their actions were wrong. They see the consequences of these actions and regret them, feeling bad that they hurt someone they care about. Their actions make them feel ashamed, because deep down, they don't align with their core values. They have a conscience and know that they've behaved in ways they're not proud of. And worst of all, they feel themselves falling in esteem in your eyes, and are sad by this.

Of course, you can be sad and upset and "sorry" without feeling any of the above. You can be sorry, to put it bluntly, that you were caught out. You can see the consequences and hate that they're happening, but you would have been happy to continue making those choices if you could be guaranteed that you'd avoid the consequences. It's the old, "sorry that you got caught, not sorry that you did it" difference ...and it's a big difference! Such a person regrets their actions not because they feel that they're intrinsically wrong, but because they're inconvenienced by the results and wish they could take them back. The discomfort is not in knowing themselves that they've violated some principles, but in that *someone else* is judging them for doing so. If they were never discovered, they'd feel very little remorse, or none at all.

I don't have to tell you which attitude is more likely to have a better outcome in the long run. But how do you know if your partner is truly remorseful?

Step one: follow your gut. You know your partner. It might feel like they're changing before your eyes, but listen to that voice inside anyway.

Step two: pay attention to the object of their remorse. What I mean is, when they speak about feeling bad about their actions, listen to *who* and *what* they're upset about. If the focus is on you, and how they can't stand to have hurt you, that's a better sign than if they focus on how terrible *they* feel for everything that's happened.

Do they speak about all the things they want you to do now, i.e. to forgive you and to let them explain etc. or do they beg you to tell them what they can do to make it better for *you*? To put it simply, is their focus on you and the relationship itself, or are they concerned with their own wants and needs first?

Condition three: your partner is committed to the practical work of earning your trust again

A partner who has cheated and feels no remorse will get impatient and want you to forgive as soon as possible, but only because *they* don't want to have to deal with their negative feelings. To relieve themselves of guilt, they might push you to understand their perspective and to get over it. In fact, you might be shocked to discover that the work seems to be all yours: they have all the fun of destroying your relationship and you have to be the bigger person and graciously forgive!

The three conditions I'm discussing here are not about revenge or taking the moral high ground. They're not about smugly looking down on our partners and enjoying the fact that they are wrong and we are right. But it is about determining your chances of saving your relationship. This is tricky to do since you are probably not feeling trustworthy of them in the least! So the solution is to not rely on what they say alone. Instead, look at what they *do*.

Has your partner *taken active, real, concrete* steps to put your relationship back in focus and start gaining back your trust?

Be careful here; a promise of what they'll do in future is just not the same thing as actually doing something. You won't fully trust them, they might break that promise anyway, and you'll be stuck in a vicious cycle where their word disintegrates in value to nothing.

Hard as it may be, and tempting as it may feel to believe the promises and hold onto *something*, ignore the words. Look at your partner's behavior instead.

If the infidelity has happened at work, for example, have they taken steps to move to another department, or deliberately talk to the other person and tell them in no uncertain terms that there will be no more contact between them? If you've discovered a secret online dating profile, was the profile destroyed instantly, with no further questions? If there's an actual full blow relationship with someone else, has this relationship been 100% terminated?

It seems crazy to think of it, but I know a woman whose husband calmly explained to her that he didn't want to tell his mistress he was married just yet, for fear of upsetting her. This is a clear indication that the person is not seriously committed to making any changes. A cheater should not only feel remorseful and be committed to telling the truth, they should be funneling their energies into their relationship – it's an emergency, after all!

Chat to your partner about whether they'll be getting STI tests, what they plan to do to cut contact with the other people involved, and how exactly they will start making your relationship a priority. If they seem resistant or surprised by these questions, again, pay attention. A truly remorseful person dedicated to making your relationship work will jump at a concrete suggestion to make things right.

Chapter 3: Radical Honesty and The Blessing of a Fresh Start

Now even I'll admit that that previous chapter is something of a downer. It's a little grim to begin such a positive book with what looks like an ultimatum, isn't it? But the reason I list those three conditions is not so that you can gloat or feel superior. It's not so that you can put your partner through the ringer.

It's so that you can *save time*.

Because the "ball is in your court", and your partner will be anxious for some kind of resolution (as will you!) you may be pressured into forgiving and moving on. But the truth is that re-building trust takes work from *both* of you. You may want with all your heart to move past this disaster. You may feel angry and hurt but still have a seed deep down that wants to try make things work and move on. That's great!

But in your faint hope and optimism, don't lose sight of the fact that you cannot save your relationship *on your own*. If it heals, it will be because of both of you. This means that if you're bravely committing to learning to trust again, and your partner has no intention of doing the same, you're needlessly exposing yourself to more hurt and disappointment.

You need to determine, right in the beginning, what the cheating really meant, and why it happened.

Some people cheat because they're sad and lonely and stressed. They make a single poor choice and regret it deeply. They see immediately how it's not what they wanted, and the experience leads them deeper into their relationships, making them more aware of what's important. They learn new things about themselves and the people they love, and embrace the challenge of making things better.

But let's be honest, some people cheat because they can. Some people acknowledge the damage it causes, and still choose to deceive those they love, for a quick thrill in the moment.

Your hard work and effort at building up trust will not be wasted with the first kind of person. But it certainly will with the second.

So figure out what's what before you decide to commit to the process of healing. As with anything in relationships, commitment from both partners is necessary. Commitment from just one is not a relationship, it's a delusion.

The great thing about infidelity is that it can be the most genuine thing a relationship experiences! I mean that. For some people, it takes the disaster of an affair to finally force them to have the conversation they should have had years ago. Cheating is nasty and unpleasant and destructive ...but it can also have a way of clearing away the crap and bringing the hard truths to light.

Together with your partner, or alone, consider the following questions very, very carefully.

Of course, asking your partner to have a look at these questions and having them resist is an answer in itself. But be curious. Listen without judgment. Your goal is to understand WHY this has happened. Not to punish and judge, but to understand. This understanding will not only give you a better idea of how to move forward, but whether or not you should be moving forward at all.

Just a warning: going through these questions can be grueling. You may dredge up information and feelings that are raw and painful and scary. Take a break if things become too intense. There's only one rule when going through these questions: be *honest*. The only antidote for deception is honesty, and the journey towards healing after infidelity starts with painfully removing the lies, no matter how many there are and how much it hurts to do so.

1. Ask them directly: why do they think they cheated?
2. What did the cheating provide that they couldn't find somewhere else in their lives?
3. Have they cheated before? For the same or different reasons?
4. Were they caught or did they confess?
5. How extensive is the deception, i.e. did this infidelity takes years of daily lies or was it a single event?
6. Was the cheating pre-meditated, or a spur of the moment mistake involving alcohol, for instance?
7. Did your partner lie to you before, even when you asked, "are you cheating?"
8. If you hadn't found out, would they have continued? Did they plan to tell you ever?
9. What is the size of the infidelity? Is it a passing flirtation or is

it a full on, long term loving relationship? Is it an inappropriate friendship, just sexual or are there strong feelings involved?

10.   Fundamentally, is your partner happy in your relationship?

11. Before you found out, what were the effects of the affair? Was your partner increasingly distant or did they maintain the same old affection for you, not changing towards you at all?

12. What does your partner actually think about the chances of them remaining faithful in future?

13. Does your partner want your relationship to stay the same as it always was?

14. Have they taken steps to remove all the conditions that caused them to cheat in the first place?

15. What have you done to push your partner away? Have you been doing everything you can to maintain intimacy? Have they?

16. Do you *want* to find trust for them again?

Just answering these questions may bring up extra trauma to deal with. Try to have compassion for yourself if you find it difficult, though. Once you've pushed through, you may discover an incredible calm settling in over you. With dishonesty, the world looks black and scary and unknown. But if you can be brave and take a good hard look at what you're dealing with, you can start to make out some shapes in the darkness, and soon, you can clearly see the full dimensions of the problem in front of you.

This can be a huge relief, I promise! And it's the first step to psychologically coming to terms with your new reality. Think of it as picking up all the puzzle pieces and laying them back on the table. You're surveying the damage. You may have lost a few pieces, forever. There may be some new, unwelcome pieces in the mix. But the first step is to look at all of it, with honesty.

Having trouble staying honest? Well, if your partner is unable to share openly and directly, consider this and what it means. Being brutally honest after years of deception may take time, and may hurt like hell at first. But your partner should be *willing to try*. If the willingness is not there, won't your own willingness be wasted?

Give yourself, and your partner, some time to process what you've discussed. Best case scenario, you're both on the same page and you both want to do what it takes to make things work. Worst case is you discover that the cheating was a symptom of a bigger problem, and one that's beginning to look insurmountable. The most likely outcome is that you'll find you're somewhere between these two extremes.

A possible outcome

After you've gone through each of these questions, and had a few honest conversations, it's time to decide what to do about it!

But before we go onto the next chapter and see what this actually looks like, I want to make a point about boundaries. Your partner has violated yours, and you're processing the fallout. This is a delicate, vulnerable time. What you and your partner do now will have ramifications that may last for years to come.

This book is written for those people who are hurt and sad and confused ...*but who want to move past the infidelity*. They want to forgive, they want to be better, and they love their partners enough to try again. This doesn't mean the violation wasn't serious ...it only means that they take their relationship seriously, too, and want to give it a serious try before calling it quits.

But there's nothing wrong with calling it quits. If you've read the first few pages and thought to yourself, "you know what, this sounds like a lot of work and I'm just not interested", then that's your prerogative. You're not less compassionate or progressive or mature if you check out and decide that the boundary violation was one step too far. In fact, there are situations where stepping away early on is the smartest, most compassionate move.

Likewise, people who push through and do the work of bettering their relationships are not in denial, they aren't doormats and they aren't desperate. They've just decided that the potential to make things right outweighs the original violation.

While you're hashing things out with your partner (or deciding whether they're worth hashing out!) try to ignore the advice and judgment of others. People have their own agendas for wanting you to stay or leave a cheating partner. But it's not about them, it's about *you*.

This book is about helping you reach the best possible outcome given the challenge of infidelity. For some people, that best outcome may be dissolving the relationship sooner rather than later. We'll speak later about mindful breakups and how to make sure that you're moving ahead with crystal clear boundaries in future. But the rest of this guide is written with the assumption that you'd like to try and heal your relationship. I'll be assuming a certain optimism on your end. But honestly? Don't be afraid to check out halfway through. Now, and later, you have the option to stop, graceful disentangle and move on. You don't need anyone's permission for that!

Chapter 4: What's Yours and What's Theirs

In a divorce, you have to start think about what belongs to who. You separate out the things in your house, the debt, the kids, your own emotional baggage. As you pull apart, you both have to remember what it's like to be individual people again. What's "yours" and what's "theirs"?

Moving on after infidelity is kind of the same. Why? Because the relationship you used to have is gone. It's over. In fact, the agreements and understandings you shared with your partner have changed completely – sure, you weren't consulted on this fact, but all the same the state of your relationship is now forever different. Essentially, you've gotten divorced. The only difference is that you're staying together after the divorce.

It may seem weird to think of your "fresh start" this way, but it does capture nicely just how profound the changes you've experienced are.

In your "divorce", you're going to be dividing up the emotional work.

The reasons for doing this will become clear the longer you try to move on after your Ground Zero moment. Let's say your partner cheats, they're broken up with remorse, promises are made, and long awkward chats are had late into the night. You feel cautiously optimistic. You've reached out a little, tentatively. Things are raw, but you're hopeful. You love each other, after all.

Then one day your partner does something mildly irritating and all of a sudden you lash out at them. A few minutes into the fight you're already dredging up the "incident". Your partner feels this isn't fair – how many times do they have to apologize for the same thing? And does their past affair have anything to do with the fact that they keep breaking the dishwasher? You, on the other hand, are incensed that you're getting told off for being angry. You *are* angry. Very angry. Are they really suggesting that you get over things just like that? How convenient for them!

You can see where this kind of thing goes. Who's "right" in this situation? No matter how heartfelt the late-night discussions and no matter how sincere the promises, eventually, a couple in this situation will encounter the hard question: whose stuff is whose?

Getting stuck in blame and resentment is the single surest way to dissolve what little trust you're able to build back up. It's important to decide *who is responsible for what* early on, so that you are not getting pulled into reliving the transgression over and over, never giving your partner the chance to move on.

On your path to healing, life will be made up of all the little things it used to be made of, except now there will be a pall of doubt and tension hanging over it. You get rid of this by deliberately choosing happiness, trust and compassion, instead of dwelling in the past. This is hard, and the subject of our next chapter, but for now, stay mindful enough to ask yourself regularly, "is this mine?"

Your "stuff"

If your first thought is, "I don't have any stuff, all of this is the other guy's fault" then know that you're deliberately engaging with that pall of doubt and tension. When someone hurts you, it's natural to place the blame at the hands of the transgressor. And yes, it is your partner's "fault" that they hurt you. But it is *your responsibility* to heal from that.

This can be a difficult concept to grasp, especially when your idiot partner breaks the dishwasher for the second time that month. They are responsible for hurting you. But you are responsible for how you manage the resulting emotions. Is this fair? No. Not at all. But the brutal fact is that human beings do hurt each other, and your reactions are your own business. Own them.

You'll soon see that demanding that your partner be responsible for soothing you is not only unhealthy – it doesn't even work! You may get suspicious one day about a text or a look or an evening they spend late at the office. Those suspicions are a natural result of the infidelity. Of course you feel that way! But what you choose to do with that is actually nobody's business but yours. If you pester your partner, don't believe their answers and demand they keep providing you "proof", you soon see that they don't have the ability to assuage your doubts anyway. Only *you* do.

At some point, you reach a wall: it's not possible to see into your partner's very soul. It's not possible to trace their every move, to know anything with 100% certainty. At some point, you have to *trust*. Not for them. Not as a reward they earn for repenting, but for YOU, because it feels better to trust and honestly, it's more practical. Living in paranoia is profoundly disempowering and crazy-making.

You're going to be sensitized and doubtful after an infidelity. Your partner has eroded your sense of trust. The world was one way, and then they yanked the carpet out from under you, and now you're wary of taking anything at face value again. And that's normal! But if you want to heal and move on ...eventually, you do have to move on. Eventually you have to disengage your own feelings from their actions.

I know someone whose girlfriend cheated on him. Their relationship went through the grinder, but they stayed together. However, things were never the same. He demanded every password and access to every social media account she owned. He read her mail, kept tabs on her throughout the day and secretly enlisted the help of others to keep an eye on her. He felt that this was a kind of "solution". His girlfriend went along with it, wracked by grief and the feeling that she deserved to be surveyed, and even punished a little. But the result was that more than a year later, they were still in the same doubtful limbo. They eventually did break up. She never cheated again, but it didn't matter – the real damage to the relationship came in the months *after* she cheated.

What went wrong? Well, I think the problem was that they were both unclear of what belonged to whom. He was torn up (of course he was!) but instead of dealing with his own emotions, he made her responsible for them. He conditioned his well-being on her "behaving". Instead of controlling himself, he controlled her. And she, instead of processing her own emotions (guilt, self-hate) she allowed *him* to process them for her by continually punishing her for a crime that was done and dusted. They both never took responsibility for their part in the dynamic, and so blame and resentment abounded. The trust was gone. The infidelity was the catalyst. But what really killed their relationship, I think, was their inability to take responsibility for their own baggage ...and refuse to carry the baggage of anyone else!

Sounds great, but how do you determine what's yours and what's theirs anyway?

Start by remembering this: *your emotions, good and bad, are your own.*

Sure, other people's actions affect us. That's kind of the point of
this book. But you are an adult, and how you behave in adversity is
your responsibility. Nobody can "make" you feel anything. If you
feel mistrustful, recognize that you are actively choosing to feed
and maintain that feeling in yourself. And that you can just as
actively choose to starve out that emotion and nurture a different
one.

I know what you're thinking: "but I can't do that! Do you have any
idea what he did to me? It's not so easy to forgive, you know!"

I know. It isn't easy. But it is necessary. This is the "work".

Think of this. If you are hurt, and you close your heart, the person
who hurt you has taken *two* things from you: they have taken your
trust in them, but they've also taken all the trust you would have
given in the future. You've also allowed them to rob you of the
ability to enjoy and trust others again, forever. Are you happy to
take that damage and dwell on it so that it takes over your whole
life?

If the hurt has taken its toll, wouldn't you rather minimize that damage? Wouldn't you rather shake it off and get back to being healthy and trusting and open as soon as possible? We sometimes imagine that allowing bitterness and doubt and resentment into our hearts will somehow punish the one who hurt us. It's a spiteful mindset, one in which we unconsciously say, 'fine, I will take my delicate self and hide it away forever, so it can't be hurt again."

But doing this doesn't punish anyone *except us*. They have hurt you. But don't allow them to also take away your natural trust and faith in other people, your curiosity, your willingness to believe that people can be good. *That* is the real damage. And it is a damage that you are complicit in creating.

What is your "stuff"? It's the sum total of your thoughts, feelings, actions and beliefs that together form your mindset. Life is unfair, but this domain is 100% under your control, always.

- Keep events in their rightful place. If you're upset with your partner about something, stick to that *specific* thing. Don't use minor arguments as an arena to fight about big, unsettled resentments.

- Don't make it your partner's problem to soothe you. They can certainly try, but deciding "I'm going to relax and trust now" is only ever up to you. Don't force your partner to produce never-ending "evidence". Don't grill them. They will behave how they behave, and you will feel how you feel. The two are actually not as connected as you think! If you feel awful, ask, "what thoughts am I holding that are perpetuating this awful feeling?" You'll likely find that the source of your discomfort is inside you, and not in something your partner is currently doing wrong.

- Own your needs and voice them assertively. You'll feel raw that your needs weren't met *in the past*. But the past is over. Have respect for your partner and express your needs, in the moment. Are you feeling sad and lonely and just want some affection? Don't get angry at your partner for not reading your mind and pre-empting your needs. Just ask!

- Forget about "closure". You may be tempted to ask for gruesome details of the infidelity or ask your partner awkward questions that you won't like the answer to. You'll convince yourself that doing this is cathartic somehow. What's probably happening, though, is that you're traumatized. A common symptom of PTSD is "re-experiencing", which means the brain wants to keep returning to the traumatic moment in a desperate bid to "make sense" of what happened. You feel that if you can just understand, just know all the nasty details, then you'll have control somehow. But let it go. Your healing lies in front of you, not behind.

Their "stuff"

Well, all of that's great and all, but what about them? Aren't they responsible for *anything*?

Here's something to hold onto when you feel yourself slipping into anger and resentment over your partner's bad behavior: it's not your stuff, it's theirs. You don't have control over what they think, how they act, or what they say. None whatsoever. You can love and trust them, you can express your needs and limits, but at the end of the day, what they choose to do is 100% their stuff ...just like yours is yours!

What stuff are they responsible for? Exactly how much are they to blame?

Well, does it matter?

Revenge and judgment can feel good. For a while. But they never lead to true healing. You might be thinking that what I'm explaining here is foolish. That if you completely stop trying to control your partner, if you give them your trust and forgive them, that you've somehow made it more likely that they'll hurt you again.

But here's the truth (and this truth may be liberating or horrifying, depending on your mindset!): *nothing that you do has any effect on whether they hurt you or not.* Really. You were not in control of them before, and you are not in control now. You may have *felt* like you were in control, before they cheated, but that was not because of something they were doing, it was because of something *you* were doing. They are no more or less trustworthy now, only your mindset towards them has changed. If someone wants to cheat on you, they will. Being extra vigilant or being caring and trusting will make no difference to whether they ultimately do it. Why? Because it's their decision, not yours.

But, being trusting will *feel* much better for you. So if it doesn't matter what you do, why not choose to do the thing that makes you happy?

If you're thinking, "because then they'll cheat on me and then I'll be the idiot who let themselves get hurt", well, here's where your boundaries come in. You don't need to be angry and spiteful to have a boundary. You can be open, trusting and light in your spirit right up until someone violates that boundary. And then, since you are in charge, you can terminate your connection. Not in anger to the violator, but in love to yourself.

You are warranted in "checking up" on your partner here and there, especially if trust has been broken. But don't torture yourself. Determine if your boundaries are being respected. Express your needs. Be kind, in the moment. *That* is your business. They can cheat on you again, sure. They can throw away your trust and act against their principles and yours. But that is *their* business.

Chapter 5: Committing After Your Trust is Gone

Healing after infidelity is a bit of a Catch-22: The only way you can heal after cheating is to *commit* to forgiving, to give everyone the chance to tell a different story and do something else. But this is precisely what you don't feel like doing!

You can't trust your partner again because they broke your trust the last time they had it. Now what?

Trust is something that builds on itself. You give a little, it works out well, you give a little more. You open up a little, your partner respects and cares for you, you open up a little more. You give, they give, you give again. Soon, you have a history and a relationship that is predictable and secure.

When your partner cheated, they smashed all your saved progress to bits. Now, to build back up again, you need that first, crucial bit of trust. The bit of trust that will allow you trust a little bit more next time, and then a little more. But someone has to "go first". Who's it going to be?

Maybe you can guess, but I'm going to say that the answer is *you*. You have to go first. More than likely, your partner still trusts you. You didn't damage their trust, and so it's still there. But now it's asymmetrical. Your trust in them is at a big fat zero. And it's "your stuff" to place that first piece down so that trust can be built up slowly again.

You may start looking for a reason to pay them that trust. We talk of trust as something people "earn". And that's true. Trust is not handed out willy-nilly, free for anyone. That's what makes it valuable. So maybe you think, has my partner apologized enough yet? Has my anger and hurt diminished enough? Have they earned me taking that first step yet?

I would like to suggest that this first piece of the trust mountain is different from the others. This first piece is not earned. It's just given. It's just an act of faith, something you give and hold thumbs that you made a good choice and that the person you gave it to will return the favor.

If you are waiting for your partner to prove themselves to you, it might work, it might not. You might wait a very long time! Whether it works or not, asking your partner to take the first step is putting yourself in a reactive frame of mind, rather than a proactive one. It might not feel like it's fair for you to take a risk and trust again since they're the bad guys, and they broke everything in the first place. But this is life. This is the grace of healing. And it can be an incredible gift – not to the cheater, but to *yourself*!

Now, I'm not a fool and I'm not asking you to be romantically and stupidly trusting right after your trust has been broken. But what I am suggesting is that you are *selectively* compassionate. Your attitude to someone who has hurt you will be different – and it should be! So here is my suggested compromise. Think of this as a way to protect your heart without shutting it down:

Give 100% of yourself, and trust completely. But do so *intermittently*.

If you don't feel 100% trusting of your partner in the moment, then don't trust. Easy. Don't close your heart, just don't open it to them, for now. Don't linger in that space, though. You don't achieve anything by being partly forgiving, partly compassionate, half in and half out. Commit to trusting when you feel strong and able. Be with your partner, in the present moment. Choose to love and trust and be vulnerable and all that other good stuff.

And when you don't, don't. Your trust "tank" is not as full as it was before. You're on emergency stores. But instead of running the tap on a low trickle, eking out what little goodwill you can for your partner, open it fully and completely. Let it flow. Immerse yourself completely and utterly in the moment and *trust*. If you can only do that for short periods, great. You gain nothing by half measures.

The reason for doing this is that it saves you from growing a new relationship built on impartial trust. You take the leap of faith and "go first". Instead of feeding your doubts, you give yourself the chance to learn what it's like to live without them. And something special happens: during those authentic, trusting and open moments with your partner, they get to put down fresh trust pieces, building up that mountain again. When you're begrudgingly giving trust little by little, your partner can only build little by little too. Stinginess of spirit begets more stinginess of spirit.

So, set the pace. Invite your partner to be kind and open with you again, and trust that they can rise to the challenge. You are not signing away your life or asking to be a doormat. You're just making that first move. It's not forgiveness yet, but it's opening a space where you can forgive. There is no need to martyr yourself. Make your move and then step back and wait for your partner to meet you there.

Chapter 6: Can You Prevent Infidelity from Happening Again?

I think I can imagine what went through your mind as you read the previous chapter. Maybe it *seems* so sweet and nice, just to trust again. But maybe you read something like that and all you can think about was being hurt again, or the sinking paranoia that your partner no longer loves you, that there can never be those same feelings of comfort between you ever again.

I get that. When you try to put back those little jigsaw pieces, you may be wincing, wondering if your partner is about to jump in and ruin it all again. Try to remember, though, that you give trust for yourself, and because it feels good to give it. You can't force yourself. You can only let go. Picture it not as something unpleasant you have to endure, but a deliberate reorienting: you loved your partner once before, and you trusted once before. It's just a matter of finding that again.

It's risky, though. And it's risky for a very good reason: you may be deceived, *again*.

Your partner may well feel like they got off easy, that they can take your trust and forgiveness for granted. They may simply cheat again.

But even here, acting in compassion and self-awareness will never lead you astray. Here's why: if your partner does cheat again, then you are in the supremely easy position of knowing with 100% certainty that you can leave. Ending a relationship can be nerve-wracking because you're not sure if it's worth saving, how much is your own fault, what can be forgiven and blah blah blah. But if this happens? It's kind of a blessing. Your partner has told you clear and plain as day that there is nothing left for you to pursue with them, and you can leave with an open heart and a clear conscience. *That* is why you give them a "second chance".

Remember, you can only control your business. If people don't respect your boundaries, it's your business to reinforce those boundaries by following through with consequences. Love freely and openly, but if your boundaries are violated – repeatedly! – then relax and know that there's nothing more you can do but remove yourself from that situation. In a way, it's the cleanest, easiest outcome. There's nothing to really think about. It might hurt like hell, yes, but letting go of someone's disrespect for you can be a surprising relief.

When you're in the process of healing and building up trust again, make some boundaries for yourself. And make sure that both you and your partner know exactly what it means when those boundaries are broken. Not everyone deserves your trust. Some people cheat over and over because they have an unconscious belief that commitment = loss of freedom. Some cheat because their self-esteem is low and they crave validation and attention. Some cheat because they are addicted to sex or thrill-seeking. Some cheat because they lack the maturity to pursue the things they want, and would rather relationships blow up than decisively end them themselves.

In any case, it's not your business *why* someone would choose to keep on deceiving you. You only need to acknowledge that they have, and that you won't let it happen again. If you start building the puzzle again with your partner, and they break it, again, then leave. Break all contact and move far, far away from that person. You will only damage yourself (and them!) by staying.

So, onto the question of this chapter: can you prevent infidelity from happening again?

This question is actually fear in disguise. It's asking, if I close my heart up in the right ways, will I be able to prevent someone from hurting me again?"

It's the wrong question. The answer to this question is easy: no. You can never change how people choose to live *their* lives. There is no trick or magic talisman that will protect you from that, ever.

But you can live your life the best way you know how. You can make healthy choices for yourself. You can set up boundaries, defend them and gravitate towards people who respect and cherish you. And then, so what if anyone cheats on you? Feel sorry for them – it's a whole separate hell to live life as a deceitful person. And they lose the trust of someone great: you!

Many of us feel that if we're slow to trust again, we can inoculate ourselves from getting hurt in the future. But this approach has its drawbacks. Getting really close to someone means allowing a degree of vulnerability. Close yourself up and you'll protect yourself from pain ...but you'll also numb yourself to all the good things, too.

You don't have to do anything special to make sure people don't hurt you. You don't need to build walls or try desperately to be better so that people will not be tempted to abandon you. The best way to mitigate the pain of relying on other people is not to pretend you don't need to rely on them, it's to say "to hell with it", and to love deeply, even though it might hurt.

Don't allow your partner's (or ex-partner's) bad decisions to warp your life. I'm talking about developing a nasty dislike for the opposite sex, or becoming cynical or shutting yourself off from any romantic engagement. As long as there are people, they will hurt one another. But so what? The cost is worth it.

If you're prone to landing up in abusive or manipulative situations, or you keep being drawn to people who (for whatever reason) don't want to commit fully to you, now's the time to do your homework and make sure you're going out into the world in "good working order", single or not:

- Take an honest look at your relationship history and the patterns there. Have you pursued people who have directly or indirectly told you that they will not prioritize your feelings or their relationship with you? Many women who are repeatedly cheated on unconsciously choose men they know will reject them, simply because this fits in with their view of themselves. If you feel like you've been begging to be someone's "number one" since you were a little girl, look closely at the ways you may be seeking out that same dynamic now. You may just need practice in what it feels like to be respected and cherished!

- Nobody deserves to be lied to. But many people cheat because their partners have shut them down, taken them for granted or denied them sex and affection for years. Ask yourself honestly if you have been nurturing your partner and making them feel cared for and wanted. Do you actively maintain the relationship or just assume it'll run on its own?

- People who cheat do not, in most cases, see their partners as *primary*. Ask yourself why this is. Try to understand your own needs and wants when it comes to commitment. Have you asked for what you need? Have you carried yourself in a way that communicates the respect you have for yourself? Many of us go into relationships just assuming that both people are on the same page when it comes to what counts as cheating, but is there a *spirit of commitment* running through your relationship? Or are you in a limbo, waiting for something? Infidelity can sometimes have the surprising result of revealing how differently people actually think of "commitment". The next relationship you're in (including version 2.0 of your old relationship!) be clear about what you expect and why.

So ...what about non-monogamy?

No book about infidelity would be complete without a consideration of monogamy, right? Well, maybe. I want to say, though, that commitment has nothing to do with the number of people in a relationship. Polyamorous people or those in open or non-monogamous relationships will emphatically say that their relationship model is *not* about infidelity. That what they do isn't "commitment-lite" or glorified cheating. In fact, commitment, honesty and responsibility are just as important in these kinds of arrangements as ever. Maybe even more so.

If you've had the thought that maybe you should "downgrade" your cheating relationship to an open one, since its already technically open, think again! Those with experience will tell you that polyamorous setups almost always fail when they begin with deception. And why wouldn't they? If you couldn't trust your partner with one set of rules and expectations, why would it work with a different set?

Of course, it's a legitimate wonder. Your partner may have cheated because deep down, they crave the affection and love of more than one person, and this has nothing to do with how much they love *you*. This is more common than you think. People are perfectly capable of forming deep, meaningful attachments to more than one person at a time.

But there is a mature and compassionate way to deal with these feelings. Many people are open and honest with their partners. They share their desires thoughtfully, and discuss them in a trusting context. And there is nothing to say that two loving, thoughtful people can't transition from a monogamous to a non-monogamous relationship. It happens all the time!

The problem is the *deception*. Whether a person identifies with the philosophy of non-monogamy or not is almost beside the point: if they've been lying to their partners, that's the most salient feature of their relationship. And cheating and lying are no easier or more natural in a non-monogamous setup.

So, will switching to an open relationship redeem your cheating partner? It's highly unlikely. If this is the way that your conversations are going, well, great. But the fact remains: the hard work of healing your connection isn't going anywhere. You have to do that work. Bringing other people into your relationship is a privilege for those who have already earned deep trust and security with one another. If you've just cheated, your relationship is nowhere near ready for that, and so it's kind of pointless to wonder whether that relationship model is right for you. Heal the trust you have with your partner first. Build it up again. *Then* you can decide on the varsity-level relationship stuff.

Chapter 7: The Truth About "Mistakes" and "Accidents"

A man goes out with friends to a bachelor's party. They're all at the groom's house, people are drinking, things are slowly getting raucous. Then the strippers arrive. This is a surprise to some of the guests, who were promised a "tame" evening. Uncomfortable, they leave soon after. Our man, however, stays. His girlfriend texts him a message to say she hopes he's having fun. He sees the message, and thinks about responding. But he doesn't.

Naturally, things get more and more out of hand. Our man sees that 1am rolls around, and remembers that he told his girlfriend to expect him home at midnight. He's quite drunk, though, and thinks, what the hell. He's already there, he's not *technically* doing anything wrong. When one of the strippers turns her focus to him and starts touching him, he feels a little guilty. But, this *is* a bachelor's party, after all. He never asked for her to do that. More guests leave, going back home to wives, girlfriends or families. Our man does not. Eventually, the stripper goes even further.

The next morning, his girlfriend is understandably livid.

Someone's put a very embarrassing picture on Facebook of our man and the stripper, and she is beyond hurt. Our man feels awful. He is sorry. "It was a mistake" he tells her. He had too much to drink, he was just there supporting his buddy, it was a bachelor's party, after all, that's just the kind of thing that happens, it meant nothing. It was an *accident*.

Now consider another man. He dates a woman for three years, and they break up because they both move to different cities. They lose touch but eventually, by some twist of fate, they end up working at the same company. Both of them are married now, but they strike up a friendship again.

One day it's a Christmas year-end party at the office and the woman is emotional, confessing to the man that she missed him terribly all these years, that she wished they had never broken up, that she might even still love him. In the heat of the moment, they kiss.

Both are wracked with guilt and cut contact immediately. Our second man goes home, confesses to his wife and tries to explain what happened. It wasn't what he intended. He loves her a lot and they were just caught up in the moment, nostalgic, a little carried away with things. It was a mistake. It was an accident.

Now, which of these cheating stories is "worse"?

Is man 1 or man 2 the more deceptive? On the surface, maybe you're tempted to say the first guy is just a bit of a moron. He got drunk, he didn't mean it to happen ...and it was a bachelor's party, after all. Looks like an innocent mistake, even if he was kind of an ass about it. Maybe you think that the second scenario sounds scarier. Here, the two in question loved each other. It just seems more serious. They're both married!

The best way to understand all the millions of ways that people can bend and test the "technical" rules of what counts as cheating and what doesn't, is to look at the intention behind the behavior. Though Man 1 claims he made an accident, in truth, he made several perfectly conscious decisions to harm his relationship with his girlfriend well before there was a stripper grinding in his lap.

He chose to ignore her texts. He chose to stay when he saw things getting heated. He chose to drink, chose to stay out later than he said he would, and chose not to mention the incident when he got home. None of this was an accident. These were actions taken that reveal an attitude of disrespect. It's the behavior of someone who hasn't prioritized his partner. To say "it's a stag party, that's just what happens" is to shirk responsibility.

If your partner has repeatedly chosen to put themselves in a situation where cheating is likely, well, don't let those choices go unnoticed. People who follow the letter of the law in their relationships have already been unfaithful in spirit. They are already looking for ways to act without consequences. The "accident" may just be the natural fulfilment of what they really want, deep down. Who knows what tempting little situations that person might repeatedly find themselves in later on?

Beware of "accidents" that happen over and over again. We are all human and having some compassion for your partner is always a good idea. We all can succumb to the attention of someone else, to the lure of a different life, of something forbidden and new and even a little dangerous. But once you make a decision in that direction, *and then keep going*, then you are no longer making a mistake. You are making poor decisions.

Cheating can be a moment of carelessness and weakness. Or it can be a manifestation of a deeper problem.

Man number 2 shouldn't have kissed his ex. But he has more right to call it an accident. Once both of them realized the line they had crossed, the situation was shut down and the other spouses were informed. It's not natural to expect that people magically stop having feelings for others the second they say "I do". "Slip ups" like this are not only likely, they're actually pretty common. But if handled correctly, they can strengthen a commitment. Both partners can see evidence of one another choosing, in each passing moment, to devote their energies to the relationship that matters, to prioritize it, and to defend it.

If your cheating story has an "accident" flavor to it, look closely and see what this actually means. Look at the *intention* behind the choices, as poor as they may be. Look at what leads up to accidents. Sometimes, negligence is worse than malice. If your partner's defense was that they "weren't thinking", ask yourself if you're happy to have your feelings so unvalued that they don't even register when you're not there to speak up.

I like to think that people, on the whole, are good. When people hurt others, most do so out of their own weakness, and when you can be kind to them, they can learn to be better. I'm a big believer in compassion. It's human to lust after others, to wonder what life would be like if you chose boy B rather boy A, to wish for a little thrill once in a while or feel the rush of being noticed by someone new.

But it's also human to want to push through those momentary distractions and remember to act according to what's *really* important at the end of the day. It's also human to want to be better than passing temptations and to commit to something bigger.

Hurting one another is par for the course. But if you are going to be compassionate with someone, look for evidence that there is a matching compassion in them, too.

Chapter 8: Exercises

If it seems like we've spent ages on the previous sections, it's only because *laying the groundwork* is so important in healing from infidelity. When your partner cheats, you're not having a problem with your relationship, rather, your entire relationship is the problem! It might seem overly-dramatic, but infidelity eats away at the most fundamental layers of a partnership. To undo the damage, you need to get right in at the root of things.

The following exercises should only be attempted once you've determined that you are both willing to do the work it takes to start building again. If you are brimming over with resentment and lauding your "second chance" over them as a form of punishment, you won't heal. If your partner is squirming away from taking responsibility and unwilling to make changes going forward, then they won't heal, either.

But if you're both courageous enough to start with a commitment to something new, these exercises can bring some order to the chaos.

Exercise one: dates with the present moment

There are going to be a few tearful and awkward conversations along the way. But that doesn't mean your whole life must become one big tearful and awkward conversation! Give yourself and your partner the chance to actually enjoy one another again, to build up a relationship that isn't defined by this awful, ground zero moment. You'll be upset, possibly for a long time, but for this exercise, put that aside just for one evening, and go on a "date with the present moment".

Do something fun with your partner. But the trick is to *not bring up the past in any way, shape or form.* Not even to reminisce or remember something good. Just be in the moment, forget about the infidelity for a second and enjoy the moment. Flirt a little, enjoy the activity at hand and try to see your partner, as they are, in front of you. Of course, you don't have to pretend that your anger and hurt and doubt don't exist anymore. But "shelve" those feelings and come back to them later. For now, just relax and enjoy.

Exercise two: create "checkpoints"

As the partner who's been deceived, you might feel the burning need to check that your partner is not still deceiving you. You might demand to see their text histories or follow them to make sure they're going where they say they go. I can promise you, these feelings are normal, but acting on them will *not* make you feel better.

You'll make your partner feel like a scolded child and you'll only reinforce your mistrust of them. And worse, if you discover that everything's fine, deep down you'll only start to wonder if they're behaving themselves simply because they know they're being watched! If you don't want a Cold War style atmosphere in your home, don't do this, to yourself or your partner.

Instead of spying on your partner or looking for "evidence", set up your lifestyle with "checkpoints" that will help soothe your doubts but won't establish a parent/child dynamic with your partner. This could be daily rituals like texts when they leave or arrive at a place, or a commitment to meeting at the same place and time every afternoon for coffee. Pick checkpoints together. They don't have to be big things, just little spots in both of your schedules where you can reach out, touch base and confirm, "yes, I'm here, everything's fine."

This gives your partner many small opportunities to be on time, to show that they're present and paying attention. These little "mini commitments" accumulate. You may even decide to keep things more open ended and tell your partner that while things heal, you need them to reach out and arrange a special meeting each and every week with you. Don't nag, don't bully, just let them know that doing so will soothe you and help you build up trust. Then wait. Give your partner the chance to show you, over and over again, that they "choose" you, that they're present and focused on you.

Whatever your checkpoints are, though, make them voluntary. You don't build up any trust by forcing your partner to confess, badgering them for details about their day, spying on them etc. You build up trust when you create opportunities for them to take care of you, and see that they choose to do that, of their own will.

Exercise three: have "give and take" jars

As we've seen, moving on after infidelity can be hard because the past and all the doubts it stirs up can taint the present, no matter how good it is. No matter how many sincere promises are made, no matter how many new leaves have been turned over, the ghost of the past lingers. This exercise is all about making sure those fears and resentments don't get the chance to get out hand.

It's normal for you to feel a range of emotions. Eventually, you *will* hurt less, and you *will* move on. But what to do in the meantime, when your partner is trying to make amends but all you want to do is tear their head off?

Here's a little way to process those horrible emotions as they bubble up, and deal with them before they have a chance to build up and undo all the hard work you've made to reconnect with your partner. Have two jars. One for you and one for your partner. Use beans, coins or other small pieces to represent trust, comfort and feelings of safety. When you begin this exercise, have your jar empty, and theirs full. This is a visual reminder: your trust will have to be earned, piece by piece, and it has to come *from them*.

Now, as the week goes on, you can move beans from your partner's jar into your own. Every time you feel that they've acted in a way that makes you feel loved, secure and happy, move a bean (or many beans) from their jar over to your jar. When they behave in ways that undermine your trust and have you feeling doubtful, move those beans back into their jar.

This is a great exercise because it captures very simply the process of give and take that you'll both have to commit to. Your partner will see that they have to do more than one or two grand gestures to win back your trust. And they will see that that trust gained is not permanent either, and can be lost at any time. The jars show us that trust is not usually a black and white thing. It comes in degrees. If you have a big store of trust earned, a few slip ups are not going to be so bad. But if you have no more beans left in the jar, a slip up suddenly becomes a very big deal indeed.

This is also a good exercise because it spares you from having endless conversations about how everyone is doing. It communicates directly what can be hard to put in words. It gives the cheating partner concrete feedback about how to win back your trust, and it gives you a sense of control and the feeling that you're expressing yourself and being heard. Keep the jars up for as long as you need.

Exercise four: sharing needs

If your partner is like most people, they probably cheated for (what
they think is) a very good reason. If you've done the work of
discussing this and taking responsibility where you need to, you
already know the reason why. It might not be something you're
happy to think about, but this exercise takes the spotlight off of you
and asks: how is your partner? Are they getting their needs met?

Try this exercise last, after you've built up at least a small store of
goodwill towards them again. Sit down with your partner. Both of
you will write down, on a piece of paper, ten of your relationship
needs. These are the things that you both require to feel happy,
safe and fulfilled in a relationship. Choose a mix of non-negotiable,
serious ones plus some that are nice to have, but not absolutely
necessary all the time.

Now, exchange lists. You each can choose three things off the list
that you will commit to making a reality for your partner. If they've
written, "I need sex at least 3 times a week" and you choose that

one, you will commit to having sex with them 3 times a week. If it feels difficult to do something new, remember that they are doing the same for you, and they are working hard to learn to do what *you* need and want to be happy.

You'll probably start with the easy ones, but don't stop there. Once you're comfortable with any changes you've made, come right back to the list. Can you commit to bringing any more to life? Some you may already be doing, but not quite enough. Ask your partner for specific details (for example, "do more around the house" might translate to doing the laundry once a week) and then get to work. While it's not a transaction, the idea is that you *both* commit to making the other one happy.

When one partner cheats, it's easy to get stuck in a "forgiveness loop" where one partner is eternally repentant and the other is sitting on a throne, pondering whether to forgive or not. But this ignores the other partner's needs. Worryingly, it ignores those needs that might have propelled them to cheat in the first place.

Just because your partner has cheated, doesn't mean they don't get to have demands on you anymore. Just because you are trying to forgive a hurt, doesn't mean that they don't have their own hurts. You will need extra care and attention as they build up your trust again, but you are never exempt from taking care of them and their needs.

Exercise five: a forgiveness meditation

"Forgiveness" is overrated. You don't forgive a mosquito when it bites you, because it means to bite you, and it wants to, and if it can it will bite you again. You simply accept that mosquitos bite and take the right measures to make sure you're protected. We live in a world that doesn't do much to distinguish between "justice" and "revenge". We think of forgiveness as a gift we give to perpetrators, something that makes us a gracious "bigger person".

This kind of forgiveness is really just about ego and power play. I think it's far better to *accept and be compassionate* than it is to forgive. You don't need to "forgive' a mosquito because it's just being what it is! Here, when I say "acceptance" I mean the ability to really see people, for what they are and not what you wish they were. It's the ability to acknowledge imperfection and the fact that as humans, we are all on our own paths, all struggling, all learning.

It's not wiping the slate clean or writing off a debt. It's just seeing people, all the bad included. Mosquitos bite. Humans hurt one another.

Here's an exercise that you can do alone, any time you feel your compassion for your partner running low. Simply sit or lie somewhere quiet where you won't be disturbed. Close your eyes and focus on your breathing; take a moment to pay attention to your body, the environment, your thoughts and feelings.

Now, picture your partner in front of you. Spend plenty of time really imagining every aspect of them. Remember their faces, their voices, their mannerisms. Try to see their *whole* person. Picture them as children, and all their little passions and disappointments. Picture their fears and hopes and dreams. See them achieving things, and failing at things. See them at their best and worst. See all of it. Can you feel a deep sense of appreciation for this person in front of you, and everything that they are? Can you feel love and compassion and understanding for this person? They are just like you! Mostly good, learning all the time, imperfect, human.

Now also picture yourself in their life. See them falling in love with you. See them together with you, two imperfect people who nevertheless love one another. See them enjoying life with you. See them cheating on you. It will hurt to think of this last part. But can you extend your love and compassion still, even to contain the fact that your partner has hurt you? Can you see that even though they have hurt you, that they are still people who deserve compassion and understanding?

Imagine that your partner's choices and behaviors are sitting off to the side, connected to them but not part of them. Can you look at their actions for all they are, while still loving your partner? Can you commit to and love *them*, if not their actions?

Imagine seeing potential futures unfolding for this person in front of you. See how they can grow and become better. See yourself in that picture, and how good it feels to be kind to another person. Forgive yourself and how you're not perfect either. Feel that compassion is endless, and that transgressions are only temporary. In your heart and mind, try to *accept*.

Conclusion

For many relationships, infidelity is the kiss of death. Depending on the details, willfully deceiving the person you claim to love is a crossed line that is difficult to uncross again. There is no point sugar-coating it: a relationship where one person cheats is one that is in serious crisis, and to heal it again is no easy feat.

But it *can* be done.

My hope with this book is that after the chaos and disruption of infidelity, you're able to stop, gather yourself and move forward with clarity and compassion. With effort and a true commitment to do what it takes to rebuild a damaged relationship, it is more than possible to turn a relationship built on deceit into one built on trust. In fact, it's possible for the lowest point in your relationship to spur on changes that make it stronger and more authentic than ever before.

No two people are the same, and neither are any two relationships. Cheating is complex and upsetting. There are no shortcuts to finding your own unique way out of the pain and mistrust that comes with infidelity. But one thing is for sure: if it can be done, it will only happen with compassion and self-awareness. And more importantly, it will happen WITH your partner.

Made in the USA
San Bernardino, CA
26 April 2017